THE BIBLE THE SINNER READS

Are You the Light of the World?

THE BIBLE THE SINNER READS

Are You the Light of the World?

Charlease Logan

Copyright Information

Sincere thanks to all my relatives, friends and others who in one way or another shared their prayers and support for me throughout the years.

A special thanks to Ken and Dayema Bosket for their encouragement, support, and assistance in the formation of this book.

Above all, I would like to give all thanks to God for His grace, mercy and favor.

Contents

Preface   9

Introduction   11

Chapter 1:   Our Conversation   15

   Questions for Self-Examination   21

   Scriptural Reminders   25

Chapter 2:   Our Conduct   31

   Questions for Self-Examination   37

   Scriptural Reminders   41

Chapter 3:   Our Character   47

   Questions for Self-Examination   57

   Scriptural Reminders   61

Conclusion   67

Afterword   69

About the Author   73

Preface

This book is written to help members of the body of Christ see the need for self-examination. Do we identify with Christ's words, actions, and deeds? What is the world really seeing as they look at us? This book invites and reminds us to take a serious scriptural look at our three C's (Conversation, Conduct, and Character).

The Bible states in 2 Corinthians 3:2 that we are "living epistles, known and read of all men." Therefore, we should know that others are reading and observing us. Our conversation, conduct and character are always being monitored by those who are seeking to observe the tangible difference between believers and the world.

Scripture also states that we are "ambassadors for Christ" (2 Cor. 5:20), representatives of His uprightness, integrity and faithfulness. We can be a good representative or a bad representative, but we must always be aware that someone is watching.

Introduction

Whether it is in a casual environment or a formal setting, conversation is critical to the expression of ones feelings, views and beliefs. The words that emerge from our mouths not only reflect our thought process, but also reveal our heart. The Bible states, "... for it is out of the abundance of the heart that the mouth speaks" (Lk. 6:45).

Conversation is the first of three C's that will be discussed in this book. Our conversations also include our tone of voice. The second segment of C's is our conduct. Without saying one word, our conduct is what the world sees and evaluates as they observe the actions of believers. Our conduct is reflected in what we do and how we treat others. The biblical book of Philippians notes the expected conduct of believers by stating, "Whatever happens, conduct yourselves in a manner worthy of the gospel of Christ ..." (Phil. 1:27, NIV).

Conversation and conduct are critical, but the third segment of the C's represents the depths of our surrender to God and His word. It encompasses the essence of who we are. In fact, conversation and conduct are byproducts of the third "C" which is our character. One can define character as a reflection of who we are and an internal/external manifestation of our core values and beliefs.

In this book, conversation, conduct and character take precedence as readers are spiritually shepherded through a process of introspection, reflection and self-examination.

The three C's are critical in allowing believers to

transform themselves into living testimonies that reflect the attributes of God. With transformation, believers can live the word of God and develop spiritual attributes that will ultimately allow them to become, *The Bible the Sinner Reads*.

We must examine ourselves and take a serious scriptural look at our three C's (Conversation, Conduct and Character).

Chapter 1

Our Conversation

"Let the words of my mouth, and the meditation of my heart, be acceptable in thy sight, O Lord, my strength, and my redeemer" (Ps. 19:14).

Our conversations play a major role in how the world views us, not just by the words we use, but also by our tone of voice, non-verbal expressions and our attitudes. Words have the power of life and the power of death (Prov. 18:21). We have to ask ourselves the question: Am I crucifying or assassinating someone's character/reputation with my words?

Controlling our conversations requires discipline, determination, self-control, personal awareness, and more importantly, the Holy Spirit working with us as we surrender to Him. Often, some of us speak without thinking. However, a word let go cannot be retrieved, no matter the intention, the amount of regret or apology. The Bible tells us to be "swift to hear, slow to speak, and slow to wrath" (Jas. 1:19). This reminds us to think before we speak. It helps us to respond rather than react and to maybe even question, "Is what I am saying necessary?"

Some people cannot handle the silence that may occur when assembling around others. Therefore, they find it necessary to initiate conversation when one is not needed. Random topics discussed may include subjects like weather, news, politics, and many times, people. Casual discussions may be negative, positive, or simply, gossip.

If talking about others is a regular part of our behavior, this could negatively affect our character.

Consequently, people will always know that they can engage us in "juicy" conversation. While gossip can be appeasing to our flesh, it can also be detrimental to our spiritual integrity.

The Bible admonishes us not to put a stumbling block or an occasion to fall in his brother's way (Rom. 14:13). When we engage in rumors, or just talk unfavorably about someone, we are placing an individual in a position to think negatively about another person. In other words, we are placing someone in a position to sin.

Unless our conversation is educational, edifying, uplifting or encouraging, our words can be used against us by those who are not Christians. The sinner is always watching.

Christian growth is evident in our conversation as we are determined to live the Christ life. When we are around others, our tendency is to become engaged in the conversation at hand, whether it is negative or positive. The natural man may continue to be a part of that conversation whether it is constructive or not. The spiritual man should change the subject or walk away if the conversation is negative.

If someone is speaking negatively, our interest in his or her conversation should be limited. One may ask, "How is this discussion going to benefit me?" Is it going to make me a better person? We ought to continue to discipline ourselves and avoid destructive conversations. Eventually others (i.e., family, friends, co-workers, etc.) will limit their dialog when they are around us due to our lack of interest.

When our conversation is uplifting and inspiring, the sinner gets a different picture and wants to hear more. Jesus said, "and I, if I be lifted up from the earth, will draw all men unto me" (Jn. 12:32). As Christians, this should be the priority of our conversation whenever possible; to lift Jesus up.

We must be careful when we speak. Whether it is to an individual or a group, in public, or in private, someone is watching. Whether it's a colleague or someone in authority, someone is watching. Whether the receiver is rich or poor; bound or free, someone is listening and affected by your words. We have two ears and one mouth; therefore, we should strive to listen twice as much as we speak.

There should not be any gossip, slander, criticism, or favoritism in the language we use. Our speech is to be "... seasoned with salt ..." (Col. 4:6), illustrating compassion, care, patience, love and kindness.

Therefore, before you speak think ahead and ask yourself, is it true? Is it honest? Is it just? Is it pure? Is it lovely and is it necessary? Does the other person really have a need to know?

"Death and life are in the power of the tongue; and they that love it shall eat the fruit thereof."

(Prov. 18:21)

Our Conversation

Questions for Self-Examination

Do you find that you are doing all of the talking and not listening when others speak?

Do you find yourself answering before someone can even finish asking a question?

Are you distracted while someone is trying to get your attention and really needs you to listen?

Do you murmur and complain? In your home, on the job or while interacting with others?

Do you react to conversations/situations or respond to them?

Are you slow to speak and swift to hear?

When you speak, do others listen?

Are you involved in gossip, criticizing, and/or condemning language?

Do you have something negative to say about everyone and everything?

Do you stir up strife and contention in your home, on the job, or at church?

Do you speak with a kind tone or does your tone and words contradict each other?

Are you assassinating/crucifying someone's character with your words?

Is your conversation full of pleasant words of wisdom (such as edification or encouragement) or do your words comprise of vulgarity, criticism, judgements or gossip?

Are you attentive in church or do you carry on conversations during the service?

"Only let your conversation be as it becometh the gospel of Christ: that whether I come and see you, or else be absent, I may hear of your affairs ..."

(Phil. 1:27)

Our Conversation

Scriptural Reminders

- "Pleasant words are as a honeycomb, sweet to the soul and health to the bones" (Prov. 16:24).

- "Set a watch O Lord, before my mouth. Keep the door of my lips" (Ps. 141:3).

- "Even a fool, when he holdeth his peace, is counted wise: and he that shutteth his lips is esteemed a man of understanding" (Prov. 17:28).

- "Be not deceived: Evil communication corrupts good manners" (1 Cor. 15:33).

- "That ye put off concerning the former conversation the old man, which is corrupt according to the deceitful lusts; and be renewed in the Spirit of your mind" (Eph. 4:22-23).

- "Wherefore putting away lying, speak every man truth with his neighbor: for we are members one of another" (Eph. 4:25).

- "Let all bitterness, and wrath, and anger, and clamour, and evil speaking, be put away from you, with all malice" (Eph. 4:31-32).

- "My lips shall not speak wickedness nor my tongue utter deceit" (Job 27:4).

- "Only let your conversation be as it becometh the gospel of Christ ..." (Phil. 1:27).

- "He that hideth hatred with lying lips, and he that uttereth slander, is a fool" (Prov. 10:18).

- "He that keepeth his mouth keepeth his life: but he that openeth wide his lips shall have destruction" (Prov. 13:3).

- "A soft answer turneth away wrath: but grievous words stir up anger" (Prov. 15:1).

- The tongue of the wise useth knowledge aright: but the mouth of fools poureth out foolishness" (Prov. 15:2).

- "A wholesome tongue is a tree of life: but perverseness therein is a breach in the spirit" (Prov. 15:4).

- "But I say unto you, that every idle word that men shall speak, they shall give account thereof in the day of judgement" (Mat. 12:36).

- "Keep thy tongue from evil, and thy lips from speaking guile" (Ps. 34:13).

- "But shun profane and vain babblings: for they will increase unto more ungodliness" (2 Tim. 2:16).

- "Death and life are in the power of the tongue: and they that love it shall eat the fruit thereof" (Prov. 18:21).

- "Whoso keepeth his mouth and his tongue keepeth his soul from troubles" (Prov. 21:23).

- "Be not deceived: evil communications corrupts good manners" (1 Cor.15:33).

- "Lie not one to another, seeing that ye have put off the old man with his deeds" (Col. 3:9).

- "Let no corrupt communication proceed out of your mouth, but that which is good to the use of edifying, that it may minister grace unto the hearers" (Eph. 4:29).

- "Let your speech be always with grace, seasoned with salt, that ye may know how ye ought to answer every man" (Col. 4:6).

- " ... If any man offend not in the word, the same is a perfect man, and able also to bridle the whole body" (Jas. 3:2).

- "Out of the same mouth proceedeth blessing and cursing. My brethren, these things out not so to be" (Jas. 3:10)

- "Wherefore, my beloved brethren, let every man be swift to hear, slow to speak, slow to wrath" (Jas. 1:19).

- "For he that will love life, and see good days, let him refrain his tongue from evil, and his lips that they speak no guile" (1 Pet. 3:10).

"But the fruit of the Spirit is love, joy, peace, longsuffering, gentleness, goodness, faith, meekness, temperance; against such there is no law."

(Gal. 5:22-23)

Chapter 2

Our Conduct

" ... Whatsoever ye do, do all to the glory of God" *(1 Cor. 10:31).*

Our behavior is a very real part of what people see when they are around us. Living in this society requires us to spend time around believers as well as unbelievers. Are your actions and conduct consistent regardless of your environment? Do you care what you say to people or how you say it? Do you share your faith with others and tell them the Good News?

God wants us to conduct ourselves with wisdom; His wisdom. He requires us to love each other. "By this shall all men know that ye are my disciples, if you have love one to another" (Jn. 13:35).

God, in His love for humanity, sent His only son to die for us. Jesus came and showed us examples of how we are to live and to love. He demonstrated God's love and how we are to treat others: Christians and non-Christians.

When we show love, we are patient, long-suffering, empathetic, helpful, giving, and considerate. We take time to listen, counsel if necessary, and encourage. We are humble, compassionate, kind hearted, showing brotherly love, not giving evil for evil. We ought to be swift to hear, slow to speak, and slow to anger (Jas. 1:19). Good conduct can develop into good habits and bad conduct can develop into bad habits. In other words, one's conduct can be your friend or your worse enemy.

We should think of some of the things/events that

may have produced habits that are not personally edifying. With the help of the Holy Spirit, our conduct can improve and line up with God's character.

Godly habits and practices are beneficial and help us to grow spiritually, for example, praying without ceasing (1 Thess. 5:17). The habit of reading, studying, and meditating on the word of God is essential so that we can be transformed by the renewing of our mind (Rom. 12:2).

We can engage in the habit of going to church, participating in Bible study and/or being part of a church ministry. We should develop good habits that help us to avoid distractions. Examples of disturbances that can pollute our mind may include the excessive use of the internet, social media and television. We have to persistently protect our "ear gates" and our "eye gates" in order to maintain a mindset free from pollutants (garbage in, garbage out). Once we begin the process of removing faulty habits, our conduct can progress more towards that of Jesus Christ.

There are times when we may be under attack. This may not be the most uplifting time of our lives, but it may be the greatest time to show good conduct despite our circumstances. We are to be wise in our responses despite adversity. This may be challenging, but even in our frustration, we must remember that the reputation of our Lord is at stake.

As we respond or conduct ourselves around unbelievers, they can be drawn into God's kingdom. We are told to "walk in wisdom toward those that are without ..." (Col. 4:5). We should show God's love, care and concern for others; striving to be living epistles that share the "Good News" of Jesus Christ. We should display to others the attributes of Christ: kindness, gentleness, humbleness, patience, etc., thus responding to adversity rather than reacting to it.

As you walk in love and wisdom, you will develop sympathetic and empathetic attributes, as well as compassionate, gentle, helpful, positive, and insightful qualities. When people receive empathy, they feel loved and cared about.

Our conduct can become habitual, good or bad, temporary or lasting. Since we are the light of the world, we have to be determined to exercise good conduct in every situation, showing the love of God at all times.

"Even a child is known by his doings, whether his work be pure, and whether it be right."

(Prov. 20:11)

Our Conduct

Questions for Self-Examination

Are you acknowledging God in all your ways?

Is prayer a routine part of your everyday life?

Do you read, study, and meditate on the Word of God?

Do you make an effort to memorize scripture?

Do you bring yourself into the presence of the Lord by listening or engaging in worship?

Do you spend time on things that do not edify your spiritual life? Are these things idols?

<u>Workplace</u>

Do you get to work on time, but to church late? Is your tardiness habitual, accidental or on purpose?

Are you committed to doing the best possible job at work?

Are you doing your work with excellence and to the glory of God, the One you are really working for?

Do you bring home items from the job without permission? Pens, pencils, documents, etc.

Do you make personal copies on the job without permission? Is this stealing?

Are you on private/personal calls when you should be working?

Do you return from lunch on time or are you consistently late?

Generosity

Do you give to those in need, i.e., those needing a ride or those needing your time? Do you offer someone a listening ear, money or food?

Do you stop to hold the door for a person that needs assistance?

Are you being empathetic and giving God's love to others; Christians and non-Christians? Are you making this attribute a habit?

Appearance

Do you feel the need to keep up with the latest styles/fashion even if it does not glorify God?

Is your dress too short or too tight?

Is your blouse too low or are your pants hanging off your backside?

Does your selection of clothing attract inappropriate

attention? Is it unsuitable for your environment?

<u>Surrendered</u>

Are you submitted to governmental authority?

Are you submitted to church authority?

Are you submitted to authorities at home or work?

Do you honor your parents, regardless of your age?

Our Conduct

Scriptural Reminders

- "Do all things without murmuring and disputings" (Phil. 2:14).

- "Set your affections on things above, not on things on the earth" (Col. 3:2).

- "But fornication, and all uncleanness or covetousness, let it not once be named among you, as becoming saints" (Eph. 5:3).

- "And be not drunk with wine, wherein is excess; but be filled with the Spirit" (Eph. 5:18).

- "And ye fathers, provoke not your children to wrath: but bring them up in the nurture (training) and admonition of the Lord" (Eph. 6:4).

- "This I say then, walk in the Spirit and ye shall not fulfill the lust of the flesh" (Gal. 5:16).

- "As we have therefore opportunity, let us do good unto all men, especially unto them who are of the household of faith" (Gal. 6:10).

- "Having therefore these promises, dearly beloved, let us cleanse ourselves from all filthiness of the flesh, and spirit, perfecting holiness in the fear of God" (II Cor. 7:1).

- "Be ye angry and sin not: let not the sun go down on your wrath" (Eph. 4:26).

- "Let him that stole steal no more: but rather let him labour, working with his hands the thing which is good, that he may have to give to him that needeth" (Eph. 4:28).

- "If any man defile the temple of God, him shall God destroy; for the temple of God is Holy, which temple ye are" (1 Cor. 3:17).

- "Flee fornication. Every sin that a man doth is without the body; but he that committeth fornication sinneth against his own body" (1 Cor. 6:18).

- "For ye are bought with a price: therefore glorify God in your body, and in your spirit, which are God's" (1 Cor. 6:20).

- "Nevertheless, to avoid fornication, let every man have his own wife, and let every woman have her own husband" (1 Cor. 7:2).

- "Ye cannot drink the cup of the Lord, and the cup of devils; ye cannot be partakers of the Lord's table, and of the table of devils" (1 Cor. 10:21).

- "Withhold not good from them to whom it is due, when it is in the power of thine hand to do it" (Prov. 3:27).

- "Therefore my beloved brethern, be ye steadfast, unmovable, always abounding in the work of the Lord" ... (1 Cor. 15:58).

- "Strive not with a man without cause, if he have done thee no harm" (Prov. 3:30).

- "For the ways of man are before the eyes of the Lord, and He pondereth all his goings" (Prov. 5:21).

- "Forsake the foolish, and live; and go in the way of understanding" (Prov. 9:6).

- "He that walketh with wise men shall be wise: but a companion of fools shall be destroyed" (Prov. 13:20).

- "The eyes of the Lord are in every place, beholding the evil and the good" (Prov. 15:3).

- "Commit thy works unto the Lord, and thy thoughts shall be established" (Prov. 16:3).

- "Whoso rewardeth evil for good, evil shall not depart from his house" (Prov. 17:13).

- "Let all things be done decently and in order" (1 Cor. 14:40).

"He that walketh uprightly walketh surely: but he that perverteth his ways shall be known"

(Prov. 10:9)

Chapter 3

Our Character

"Let your light so shine before men, that they may see your good works, and glorify your Father which is in heaven" (Mt. 5:16).

"...I shall be satisfied, when I awake, with thy likeness" (Ps. 17:15).

Our character is a composite of who we are, our lifestyles, how we see ourselves, how we view others, and how others see us. Character is a fixed predictable image of self-imposed discipline that others can see in us. Our conversation and our conduct help make up our character.

While we are growing from "babes" to "mature" Christians, our character should develop into Christ-like character. The absolute belief in a system of right and wrong, combined with the will to do what is right, regardless of the cost. It's a "heart" matter.

Spiritual character is formed by our commitment to Christ as well as our surrender to and love for God. When we are "in love" with Him, we seek to develop His character and subsequently become the light, a "living epistle". This is what God expects from His followers, His children.

Character can be learned. However, in order for this change to be internalized, we must make a commitment to engage in a constructive process that will develop spiritual discipline. Our conduct and conversation helps us in the development of our character. Attitude, integrity, disposition, and moral fiber are all part of an intricate building process. Character is a picture of who we really are and this is what people observe. It reveals a portrait of our lives as Christians. What do they see when they see you?

Our character is formed by our commitment to Christ and His love for us. Once we surrender to Him, we allow the Holy Spirit to grow us, teach us, and flow through us. We become disciplined in our motives, actions, and faith. As we seek His presence, pursue His word, consistently pray and grow daily, a conversion process takes place transforming us into the individuals that God wants us to be. The transformation process leads to a renewing of our minds. Then, as followers of Christ, our character will reflect Him and His call on our life.

Character reveals what the sinner sees in us. Our character traits speak for us. It is essential for us to allow godly character to develop internally so that God's love can be reflected externally. The book of Colossians emphasizes these qualities: "Therefore as the elect of God, holy and beloved, put on the tender mercies, kindness, humility, meekness, longsuffering; bearing with one another, and forgiving one another ..." (Col. 3:12-13, NKJV).

Love Traits

"Love suffers long and is kind; love does not envy; love does not parade itself, is not puffed up; does not behave rudely, does not seek its own, is not provoked, thinks no evil; does not rejoice in iniquity, but rejoices in the truth; bears all things, believes all things, hopes all things, endures all things. Love never fails. But whether there are prophecies, they will fail; whether there are tongues, they will cease; whether there is knowledge, it will vanish away." (1 Cor. 13:4-8, NKJV).

Love seeks to rapidly heal and restore. True love remains even in the worst of situations. Pure love is the highest quality of all virtues. Real love seeks to exalt the truth and does not compromise scripture. Love is not easily offended or bad tempered, yet it is quick to forgive and is never ill-mannered.

Let us wrap ourselves in love. True Christ-likeness is found in the essence of the perfection of love. When love is at the heart of our character and personality, other traits associated with love will automatically follow. These include:

Honesty: Commitment to what is true and doing only what is right.

Integrity: A sincere heart that can be trusted even when no one is watching.

Virtue: Delight in obeying God's word; being a light to others and showing perseverance.

Courage: The boldness to do what is right, take a stand and walk by faith, not by sight.

Endurance: Always ready and willing to persevere. Never getting tired of doing what is right. My eyes are fixed on Him in order to live my purpose.

Patience: Our willingness to wait on God and His perfect timing.

Wisdom: Meditating on God's word and living it. Studying, developing spiritual insight and seeing things through God's eyes.

Joy: Profound heart contentment that comes from obedience to God.

Meekness: Honoring others more than myself.

Temperance: Not allowing my senses to control or reign. Doing things in moderation.

Sincerity: People can see that my motives are pure. This attribute comes from living a life that pleases God.

Obedience: Doing all of God's Word.

Resourcefulness: Wise and creative use of all God has entrusted to us.

Quietness: Stillness in God's presence; a heart at peace.

Zeal: Eagerness to uplift God's kingdom in all I do.

Unity: Sharing God's heart in fellowship and exalting Him. Bearing one another's burdens.

Diligence: Faithfulness and endurance to complete the task and getting it done.

Excellence: Pursuit of God's plan and doing all as unto the Lord.

Yielding: Surrendering my plans to God and doing His will.

Alertness: Aware of things that might hurt others.

Empathy: Reaching out to others. Showing compassion, loyalty, caring, comforting and kindness.

Loyalty: A commitment to God's word, His people and what is right.

Mercy: Compassion and forgiveness shown in others instead of retribution. A vital part of godly character and one of the greatest virtues from God.

Humility: The ability to be humble and defer oneself for the benefit of others. Most essential of all virtues before God. Meekness and humility helps keep our ego and tongue under control.

Faith: Believing in what we cannot see while trusting in God, His promises, and His faithfulness. An essential aspect of the true character of the believer. It establishes a framework and foundation for every other virtue.

All of these traits are expressions of love. Without love, all good works are without merit. It is up to us to express them as a part of our character. Authentic love shows concerns for the needs of others. This is Christ-like character.

When we say that we follow Christ, our actions must show others that we do. Our character is that of Christ, therefore our words, deeds, lifestyle, and relationships ought to reveal that we are the light and expression of Christ. This ought to be our goal and mission as we become more mindful of how God's character is reflected in our lives.

"And be not conformed to this world: but be ye transformed by the renewing of your mind that ye may prove what is that good, and acceptable, and perfect, will of God."

(Rom. 12:2)

Our Character

Questions for Self-Examination

Do you love the Lord? Do you honor and respect the Lord? Do you keep His commandments?

Is prayer a routine everyday part of your life? Do you set aside time each day to pray?

Are you being transformed daily by the renewing of your mind?

Are you willing to step out in faith, even when your faith has been challenged?

Are your up one day and down the next?

<u>Thankfulness</u>

Do you have a thankful heart, a grateful heart and a pleasant personality?

Are you grateful to God for His mercy, grace, provision, and protection in times of trials and affliction? Alternatively, are you grateful in the good times only?

Do you give God a tenth (tithe) of your income and a tenth of your time (24-hour day)?

Are there idols in your life such as the job, the TV, the cell phone, internet, and social media? Is your time with God in competition with these?

<u>Family</u>

Are you in love with your spouse? Do you show that love? Are you faithful to your spouse?

Are you showing love to your children? Are you spending quality time with them?

Do you provoke your children to wrath or do you encourage them with love?

Are you training up your children according to scripture? Are you praying with them and teaching them the Word of God?

Hospitality

Do you pray for others? Are you selfish in your prayers and only pray for yourself?

Are you praying for all people and for those in authority?

Do you reach out in love to that Christian sister or brother needing food, clothing or a place to stay? How about to the non-Christian?

Do you visit those in the hospital, nursing home or assisted living facility?

Do you hold the door for the person behind you or assist someone who requires physical assistance?

Do you speak to people in passing or do you greet only those who speak to you?

Your Heart

Are you envious of others?

Are you holding unforgiveness in your heart?

Are you holding on to unconfessed sin?

Do you get angry, try to take revenge or get even?

Is lying part of your character? Do you lie against your family, friends or neighbor?

Are you a respecter of persons, respecting some and disrespecting others? Do you respect yourself?

Do you love your neighbor, yourself, and your enemy?

Do you contribute to others, ministries, and/or charities?

Are people seeing you as the light of the world?

Our Character

Scriptural Reminders

- " ... Thou shall worship the Lord thy God, and Him only shalt thou serve" (Lk. 4:8).

- "Bring ye all the tithes into the storehouse, that there may be meat in mine house ..." (Mal. 3:10).

- "Honor the Lord with thy substance and with the first fruit of all thine increase" (Prov. 3:9).

- "But the fruit of the Spirit is love, joy, peace, longsuffering, gentleness, goodness, faith, meekness, temperance: against such there is no law" (Gal. 5:22-23).

- "You are my friends if you do whatsoever I command you" (Jn. 15:14).

- "Now then we are ambassadors for Christ, as though God did beseech you by us: we pray you in Christ's stead, be ye reconciled to God" (2 Cor. 5:20).

- "For all the law is fulfilled in one word, even in this: Thou shall love thy neighbor as thyself" (Gal. 5:14).

- "Ye are our epistles written in our hearts, know and read of all men" (2 Cor. 3:2).

- "When a man's ways please the Lord, he maketh even his enemies to be at peace with him" (Prov. 16:7).

- "Let the word of Christ dwell in you richly in all wisdom; teaching and admonishing one another in psalms and hymns and spiritual songs, singing with grace in your hearts to the Lord" (Col. 3:16).

- "Therefore to him that knoweth to do good, and doeth it not, to him it is sin" (Jas. 4:17).

- "Study to show thyself approved unto God, a workman that needeth not to be ashamed, rightly dividing the word of truth" (2 Tim. 2:15).

- "The heart of the righteous studieth to answer: but the mouth of the wicked poureth out evil things" (Prov. 15:28).

- "For you see your calling, brethren, how that not many wise men after the flesh, not many mighty, not many noble are called" (I Cor. 1:26).

- "But as it is written, eye has not seen, nor ear heard, neither have entered into the heart of man, the things that God has prepared for them that love Him" (1 Cor. 2:9).

- "And now abide faith, hope, love, these three; but the greatest of these is love" (I Cor. 13:13 NKJV).

- "Examine yourselves, whether ye be in the faith; prove your own selves. Know ye not your own selves, how that Jesus Christ is in you, except ye be reprobates" (II Cor. 13:5).

- "I therefore, the prisoner of the Lord, beseech you that ye walk worthy of the vocation wherewith ye are called" (Eph. 4:1).

- "As ye have therefore received Christ Jesus the Lord, so walk ye in Him" (Col. 2:6).

- "For ye are dead, and your life is hid with Christ in God" (Col. 3:3).

- "But now ye also put off all these; anger, wrath, malice, blasphemy, filthy communication out of your mouth" (Col. 3:8).

- "Put on therefore, as the elect of God, holy and beloved bowels of mercies, kindness, humbleness of mind, meekness, longsuffering" (Col 3:12).

- "Forbearing one another and forgiving one another, if any man has a quarrel against any ..." (Col. 3:13).

- "And above all these things put on charity, which is the bond of perfectness" (Col. 3:14).

- "And whatsoever you do in word or deed, do all in the name of the Lord Jesus, giving thanks to God and the Father of Him" (Col. 3:17).

- "Let all things be done decent and in order" (1 Cor. 14:40).

- " ... Thou shalt love the Lord thy God, and Him only shalt thou serve" (Lk. 4:8).

- "If ye love me keep my commandments" (Jn. 14:15).

- "A good name is rather to be chosen than great riches, and loving favor rather than silver and gold" (Prov. 22:1).

CONCLUSION

"Let us hear the conclusion of the matter: Fear God, and keep His Commandments: for this is the whole duty of man" (Eccles. 12:13)

As children of God, we are to love the Lord with all of our heart. With that love, we are committed to obey His commandments.

Unfortunately, the commitment part is not there for everyone. We say He is Savior and Lord, but is He really Lord of our lives? When we make decisions to do things our way, are we deciding to assert control and be our own lord?

Scripture reminds us that we are "ambassadors for Christ" (2 Cor. 5:20); representatives of His character and faithfulness. The choice is ours to be an upright model of God's love or a reflection of qualities that do not coincide with His values. We should always be aware that someone is observing our conversations, conduct and character.

My prayer is that we would be determined with a zeal to do the work Jesus left for us to do, fulfill it to His glory and reflect His righteousness. If we take time to allow our three C's to develop and live the word of God, those who observe our actions may be led to seek God with all their hearts and live a life that reflect His love. Eventually, the sinner who is watching us may begin to desire some of the same qualities we exhibit, seek to learn more about Christ, and want to be a Bible the sinner reads.

God Bless.

Afterword

Prayer of Salvation

Someone may say I don't know anything about this Lord or this Jesus and what He wants from me. For those who have not accepted Jesus as their Savior and Lord, the question arises, "Have you ever taken the time to think about what will happen to you when you die?"

Once you have accepted Jesus as Savior and Lord, you have secured your place in heaven. Romans 10:9-10 states, "That if thou should confess with thy mouth the Lord Jesus, and shalt believe in thine heart that God hath raised him from the dead, thou shalt be saved." The book of Romans confirms the power of confession by stating, "For with the heart man believeth unto righteousness; and with the mouth confession is made unto salvation."

The book of Matthew states, "But seek ye first the kingdom of God, and His righteousness; and all these things shall be added unto you" (Matt. 6:33). The beautiful thing about God's love is that it is not His will that any should be lost. Therefore, if you have not made this confession of faith, repeat this prayer of salvation out loud.

Jesus, I believe that you are the Son of God. I believe that you died on the cross for my sins and that you rose from the dead. I repent of all of my sins. Please wash all my sins away and make me a child of God. I give my life to you today. Fill me with your Holy Spirit and show me how to live a life of gratitude and love for you.

If you repeated this prayer aloud and said it with a truly sincere heart, you are saved from your sins.

WELCOME TO THE FAMILY OF GOD!

As you develop your walk with God remember to trust in the Lord with all thine heart; and lean not unto thine own understanding. In all thy ways acknowledge Him, and He will direct thy paths" (Prov. 3:5-6).

Prayer Scripture

That ye might walk worthy of the Lord unto all pleasing, being fruitful in every good work, and increasing in the knowledge of God;

Strengthened with all might, according to His glorious power, unto all patience and longsuffering with joyfulness;

Giving thanks unto the Father, which hath made us meet to be partakers of the inheritance of the saints in light:

Who hath delivered us from the power of darkness, and hath translated us into the kingdom of his dear Son:

In whom we have redemption through his blood, even the forgiveness of sins.

(Col. 1:10-14)

ABOUT THE AUTHOR

Born in South Carolina, Charlease Lannette Logan has been called to be an evangelist and is led by God to spotlight the advantages of Christian living. Her heart for those in need is only surpassed by her love for God. As a single woman and child of God, her goal is to reach out to Christians and assist them in developing a passion for the things of God. Her objective is to proclaim that Jesus is not just our Savior, but Lord over every aspect of our lives. Winning souls for the Kingdom of God is the crux of her purpose. Logan's vision for all believers is that they will spiritually fortify themselves so that we who say we are Christians would be real followers of Christ.

THE BIBLE THE SINNER READS

Are You the Light of the World?

clanettelogan@gmail.com

NOTES

NOTES

www.ingramcontent.com/pod-product-compliance
Lightning Source LLC
Chambersburg PA
CBHW071844020426
42331CB00007B/1844